FRUIT OF THE SPIRIT SERIES

Snookums

Vol 1

&

The Fruit of Love
Say NO to Offense!

Dr. June Dawn Knight

www.drjune.org

ISBN-13: 978-1532723032

ISBN-10: 1532723032

DEDICATION

This series is dedicated to my father, Clinton B. Carpenter. In this picture he is with his brother Troy. They sang country music.

He passed away on January 12, 2000. I want to remember the great memories we had together.

He told my siblings and I stories of a character named Snookums. Snookums was always mischievous and we laughed so hard listening to dad's imagination. So, the Lord gave me instructions in a dream to create a character in this series named Snookums. He is very curious as he learns the fruit of the spirit and builds a better relationship with his Creator!

ACKNOWLEDGMENTS

I thank the Watson family in Springdale, Arkansas for their children's input in these books. There are five children in this home and they all know the fruit of the spirit!

Alissa, Nick, Mason, Ahna, & Audrey.

Also, I present this series to my wonderful grandchildren, Daniel, Matteo and Caleb. Nana loves you!

Strawberry Represents the Fruit of LOVE

Meet Snookums

Snookums is about eight (8) years old and recently got saved. He does not understand about the fruit of the spirit. So, in this book he will learn about the LOVE fruit

One Day Snookums wanders into the Garden and notices the tree with strawberry fruit hanging off of it.

Once upon a time there was
a very happy tree in the Garden.
People loved eating off of that tree
because the sun always shined on it and
it produced much fruit for its Creator.

Then one day an arrow came flying towards the tree with the word "offense" on it. The tree recognized it was from the mean devil so the tree pushed its branch out and screamed, "I forgive!" And the arrow turned around and left the tree. The tree continued smiling.

The arrow came back BIGGER this time, and it said, BIG OFFENSE. The tree knew that this arrow hurt his heart. He thought about it a minute then did not throw his branches out to stop it. He allowed the arrow to pierce his heart. It made a big hole in the tree's bark and exposed his heart to the devil.

L♥VE

◆◆◆◆◆◆◆◆◆◆◆

Snookums, when a heart is full of love, it is beautiful in God's sight. It is tender and soft to God. It is the way that we love people. When our heart is clean and pure, we are able to love people like God loves them. The devil does not want us to love people like that so he comes after us through offense to clog up our clean heart and to clog up our pipes to the roots of our trees. Humans are like trees to God,

We bear much fruit for Him or our roots can damage us. Watch how the tree reacts to this BIG OFFENSE.

When the arrow hit the heart of the tree, a black spirit came out of the bottom of the arrow. It traveled down the trunk of the tree. The roots that were flowing so beautiful in the rivers of living water from Heaven, now got CLOGGED UP because of this spirit!

The devil wants to clog up all of your roots which are connected to Heaven so that he can destroy the LOVE that comes out of your heart! After the tree opened up its heart to the BIG OFFENSE, the devil sent all kinds of other arrows to kill the tree. It began to make the tree an angry tree.

**One Offense.
Two Offense.
Three Offense.
The list goes on.**

The OPPOSITE OF LOVE is HATE. How do we hate someone? By getting offended. Once we open the door to one and do not forgive, it opens up to hate.

Offense clogs up our heart and begins to make it black. Our fruit on the tree dries up and it becomes a rotten tree.

Once they become a rotten tree, their heart became like a stone and was very hard to God. They did not want to be around Him anymore so he left the Garden and began hurting other people because that tree was so sad in his heart.

See how offense kills you?

Snookums, that's how offense will destroy a heart. You must walk in LOVE towards other people. We must be willing to forgive at all times.

You mean it keeps no record of wrong?

That's right! We must forgive others as Jesus has forgiven us! This is LOVE. Love forgives and has mercy on others.

That's hard to do because I want to bark at them.

The Fruit of the Spirit

Love – Strawberries

Strawberries are red like the blood of Jesus that cleanses us. They are sweet like salvation on our lips.

Joy – Pineapple

Pineapple is the symbol of hospitality. A pineapple is like a house with many doors. All the different sections that make up a pineapple is like how God wants us to open our doors of hospitality towards others.

Peace – Watermelon

Eating a piece of watermelon reminds us of the peace that God wants us to receive. Often when we eat watermelon on a nice hot summer day, it brings peace in our hearts with the sweet taste.

Patience – Lemon

A lemon is a symbol of patience. You have to eat it slowly because of its sour taste. Patience is trusting God to move even when life throws us a sour lemon. We wait patiently on the Lord.

Kindness – Grapes

Grapes are on a vine and it reminds us of Jesus. He is the vine for us and we must be kind to others even when they don't deserve it. This is how Jesus did as He died on the cross.

Goodness – Bananas

Bananas remind us of God because they hang on a tree and are encased in a beautiful coat and just waiting for its master to pull back the layers.

That's how we are with God, we wait as He pulls back the layers to our heart to reveal the sweetness.

Faithfulness – Cherries

Cherries grow on a stem together and represent double blessing. When you are faithful to God, His reward to you will be double for your trouble. He is faithful.

Gentleness – Peach

Just as the peach bruises if you're not gentle, so is other people's spirits.

Self-Control – Apple

We relate Adam and Eve as eating the apple in the Garden of Eden. They did not have self-control.

Made in the USA
Middletown, DE
03 April 2022

63547631R00015